The Territory of Rain

Also by Elizabeth Rimmer

Wherever We Live Now
(Red Squirrel Press, 2011)

THE TERRITORY OF RAIN

Poems

Elizabeth Rimmer

RED SQUIRREL PRESS

First published in the United Kingdom in 2015
by Red Squirrel Press
www.redsquirrelpress.com

Red Squirrel Press is distributed by Central Books Ltd.
and represented by Inpress Ltd.
www.inpressbooks.co.uk

Designed and typeset by Gerry Cambridge
gerry.cambridge@btinternet.com

A CIP catalogue record is available from the British Library.

ISBN: 978 1 910437 21 6

Printed in the UK by Martins the Printers Ltd. on
acid-free paper sourced from mills with FSC chain
of custody certification.
www.martins-the-printers.com

Contents

I: WALKING THE TERRITORY

For Blue,
all my love, always

I

WALKING THE TERRITORY

Oh, heart,
why can't you learn
that there is nothing to do in the world except live in it?

—Kerry Hardie from 'Helplessness'

The Territory of Rain

This is the territory of rain.
It is king here, more than cold or wind,
and all living is by negotiation
with flows and falls of water.

Earth and sky are heavy with it.
Peat grips it like a miser's fist.
River runs muddy as rain sloughs
the silt from bank and hillside.
It winks between grass stems,
silvers pot-holes in the tarmac,
attacks roofs with soft persistent fingers,
slips like sorrow between slate and timber.

And yet, the heart lifts at the sound
of falling water. It ripples
and sings like a lullaby,
even when the river is at the doorstep,
even when the soaked ground
gasps for breath and roots begin to rot.

It is king here and we serve it
with macs and umbrellas,
catch its least drips in water-butts,
watch it punch small holes in ponds,
delighted, even as we wish it elsewhere.

Walking the Territory

In this place I write
here, and here only,
to know this egg-shell,
fern frond, worm-cast,
this cloud, blanket-stitched with sunlight,
this river, its dimples and eddies.

In this place I write
this now and never again moment,
this here, new-known,
known over and over again,
the depth of it, the wealth,
the complex intensity.

In this place I write
the dialogue we hold with the earth,
a continuous exchange
of love and fruitfulness,
almost, never quite, unconscious,
grounding, creating
the landscape of home.

In this place I write
this terrain—how water shapes it
through rain stored up in peat banks,
the weight of ice, its grinding slowness,
how rivers swell and drain,
lay down and shift the sand and clay,
build and transform.

In this place I write
these rocks—igneous, sedimentary,
basaltic, overlaid, broken,
weathered gold and grey—
the big lump of Ben Ledi,
the sweep of Abbey Craig,
the folds and hollows of the Ochils,
the waterfalls, the mills,
the silver mines and spoil tips
greening over dust and slag of coal.

In this place I write
the slow growth of moss and lichen,
the wear and the interchange,
the melting, dissolving.

In this place I write
this grey of sky and how
it gives rich lustre to the green,
makes the air soft and mild.
The leaf here is not outshone
by blossom on the apple.

In this place I write
with inwardness and attention,
the meaning and the purpose
quietly growing
from deep understanding—
a poetics of blood and earth and fire.

In this place I write
to make from this here
and this now a poem,
a silken clue to thread the maze,
feel the thrum of other hands
touching, laying hold of it,
taking the weight together,
lifting it into the light.

Ice Patterns

On the choked river, shelves and reefs of ice
cling to the worn contours of mud-banks,
or fall and splash into the stream. On sunny roads
the tarmac rises cracked through slush and grit.

A bead of melt-water slips like a mouse
through the glittering air-space on the roof
between slate and the draining lumps of ice crust,
like stranded jellyfish, humped and glassy.

Ice-watcher too, Thoreau saw Walden Pond's
thick pelt carved up with axes, stripped,
harvested, stacked between boards and straw
to freshen June's mint julep and iced tea.

I love the way he noticed air in ice flow
in drifts of trapped bubbles and thick cells,
the changing levels of water, and the spring-time
blooms and swells of sand in the warm currents.

Earth must be less static than it seems.
It draws us. Bonded where we live like sheep,
hefted to our hills by observation,
we make our homes here, and are made by them.

Grounded

The wind swings round to north of west,
and cold in it catches like a roughened nail
on the glib satin fabric of this spring afternoon.

I study soil and think of the pale pasty stuff
of the fields with never a weed or a worm in it,
only a few sullen crows lifting their barbed wire feet
between the new wheat stalks. No hares now,
or curlews, and skylarks fewer and arriving late.

On the riverbank, soil is an invertebrate fizz
and ferment of squirm and wriggle. Oystercatchers
peep and nose the mud, hold late-night sessions
of whistling and mending imagined fences.
Heron stalks there, listening to rumours
of kingfisher's blue electric flypast.

In the gardens the soil is deep and dark
and full of broken china, rubble of half-bricks,
the bowls of clay pipes. As I dig the onion bed,
seeds from other gardeners, poppy, marigold,
columbine and wild pansy, come to light, and flower
between my untidy aspirations.

Recidivist gardener, neither first here,
nor last, I leave seeds too—borage, nasturtium,
blue-flowered alkanet. I am grounded here,
roots in this earth. They'll never get rid of me.

Leny Falls

Rocks are piled up everywhere, lined up drunkenly like books across a table, scooped out like spoons by falling water, lifted and dropped by glaciers. Some have parallel horizontal grooves left by the grinding of moving ice; others have cracked from top to bottom in the alternations of sun and frost. Two of them are curved over and curled into each other like a pair of very old clasped hands. On the levels, moss, lichens and blueberry have crept over them, trapping water in their matted roots and allowing soil to build up in the gaps, so that gradually they have been covered by a thick intensely green pelt. The river divides here into bright winking trickles, winding through smaller stones and layers of pebbles, flat and grey and spilled over the ground like coins. Where it slows, muds collect, furry with algae and shadowed by sodden roots and rotting stems, and the sand-brown slither of baby newts.

Butterfly orchid's
sudden shining, like a star
on the hill's wet rock.

Explaining a Few Things to Neruda

You will ask why my poetry
speaks of leaves and green rivers
and that family of goosanders
spinning and diving and drifting downstream
on the ebb tide this rainy morning.

Where are the unemployed? you ask,
the litter, the broken windows,
graffiti curse-words and allegations,
the lost generation, the hope of revolution?

You will ask why my poetry is so pretty,
all those woodlands and winter skies,
when jobs are scarce and art is strangled
and freedom is bought and sold with oil.

In those fields we have no lapwings,
no hares, a stillness of yellow rape,
and wheat after barley after wheat.
The skylark song is quenched in rain.
The moon rises over green absence.

Once there were bitterns in those reeds—
salmon, kingfisher, tufted duck,
children at the village school—all gone.
We wash the guilt of extinction off our hands.
Oh, see, the blood of extinction on our hands!

Sparrow Flock

They look, as they cling to pampas plumes,
like swollen leaf-buds or weights on fishing lines.

They slide along branches like fingers
ruffling spent orchard blossom.

They clothe the sycamore in scallywag moves
and chirpy chat, pushing in, falling off branches.

In flight, each moves by turns
from rim to hub, expendable to central,

then all turn at once on a wisp of wind
suddenly sideways in a flash-mob flicker,

a flock of drab brown and grey wings
all dust and mud, vanishing against the light.

Northern Stones

Where a truce can be made with the wind, new houses on the islands hold a parley between stone and light. In the twenty-hour days, light-wells, casements and sunrooms make a bright haven for northern summers, raked and shaken by the blasts off the sea. But the old drystone dikes, stacked as if haphazardly along the land's contours, cupped in the hill's folds to gather sheep for dipping and shearing in summer, or for shelter when the snow comes, will have no truck with it, obdurately hold the line. The grooved sea-cliff has been nibbled away by wind and water, weathered and carved into gloups and stacks and skerries, and the land behind is littered with shale and flat stone scraps. Very little grows here. Erratics have drifted across the scree. Perhaps some of these heaps are deliberate—cairns, maybe, or the first attempts at homes. It's hard to tell. Even the broch looks like the natural accumulation of stone, only these stones are bigger, heavier, much more regular. It takes a while to recognise it as a dwelling place, until the archaeologist reveals the ashy spreads around the newly uncovered hearth. There is a north wind. Earth's stone hackles quiver. Nesting birds are making their homes in what is left of ours.

Sea pink on the cliff,
a bright feminine ruffle
on grey tweed scree

Blanket Bog

Blanket bog clothes the land
like a black melancholy, shrouding
the slopes in the weight of its slo-mo layers.
Grudges and peat break down slowly.
Bones of old loves and hates
are kept intact for ever.

Sphagnum can absorb
twice its own weight in tears.
Crazy insectivorous plants
thrive on trapped flies and imagined slights,
and lost birds wail, raking through pools
and stirring the endless mud.

Keep it safe, keep it undisturbed.
Under these tons of peat and apathy
enough carbon is sequestered
to melt the last chips of polar ice
and burn up every one of us
on the whole raging earth.

River Calendar

A *House for Winter*

The sky opens blue windows
between shutters of grey cloud.
Winter peers in.

Brittle sunshine slants
between skeletonised trees,
thin relict leaves at twig tips.

A breath of frost melts
on the cold frame, split curls
of seedpods glued to the glass.

The dark glassy river is choked
with panes of broken ice,
curdled with falls of new snow.

The warm pigeon-feathered hollow
between railway bridge and river,
is a pot a-bubble with soft coos.

A white snow-mist climbs
the black walls of the hill.
Winter settles in.

Frozen Out

Frost in the ground locked tight
as a held breath. It needs
the sun's warm touch to make
meltwater pool, till earth
gasps and inhales the wet
like oxygen, and breathes
new sap into starved grass.

Bride's Chickens

Harbingers of spring,
the sound of oystercatchers
whistling in the dark.

The Harbingers

Sun combs the garden
disentangling witch hazel's
tight yellow ribbons.

The curlew's first spring song
rises from the mud, faint as river mist.
Like dragon-fly wings it strengthens,
brightens in the budding sun.

Something is opening in the air
when you walk out in the morning.
Something has arrived. A new voice
singing. The world is different.

Cutting Free

Rain on the west wind
hammers into slates
a fluid steel curtain.

The young poplar is down
settling into the loose mud.
Each tide coats it with new silt
loosens its roots a bit more.

On the riverbank lie
thinned saplings, scarred stumps,
a mess of sawdust and chippings.
Air and light strike to the roots.
It looks like butchery.

The Quickening

First rain for a month
The earth darkens, releases
the green smell of spring

Wood violets blossomed overnight,
eight sudden blue flowers
scentless and fragile on wiry stems.

On spring river banks
a hazy cloud of sallows
yellow catkin sparks

Celandines light yellow candles.
The woodpecker blazes through the trees,
Strikes home, bores deep.

Primroses, clotted cream
on a green dish of new leaves,
thicken in the sun.

The wind is backing south-westerly.
I scan the fresh April sky
watching for swallows.

Blurred

Air quivers with rain.
The Ochils hide behind
walls of new leaves.

Spring Tide in May

Wren song. The new moon rises early,
and the river races upstream,
green and leaf-flecked. Willows
shed pollen into the water.

The south-west wind
full of lime-flowers and bees
has blown the cherry petals
to a dense carpet on the grass.

Sun and shadow play kiss chase.
Welsh poppy and kingcups
light the pond's dark water. Woodruff
burns silver in the birch tree's shade.

In the hedge, a dunnock,
blue-tits and chaffinches sing.
A goldfinch is high up somewhere,
and a continuo of blackbird and thrush.

The garden is a green box
full of brown gaping fledglings.

Skygate

Dawn. Beyond the orchard
a door to a new country
a wisp of blue mist

The sky brightens in the west
ripens the white moon's fruit
from pear to peach to strawberry.

Against a shining sky
a grimy thumb-print of cloud
smudged along the hill-top.

in the garden pond
magpie in black and white
dipping for tadpoles.

Summering

Summer is moving on.
The train cuts through verges
of foxglove, rose and elderflower.
Moon-daisies burn like bonfires.
Yellow spikes of broom spill
scent of butterscotch and coconut.

Summer is loud and flirty,
all trills and cascades of birdsong
and exhibitionist butterflies
twinkling over the cuckoo flower.
Lapwings jazz-dance, and skylarks
climb the sky, lost in the sundazzle.
Swifts careen round the chimneys,
boy-racers on edgy black wings.

Summer is changing weathers,
rain and wind make kaleidoscopes
of cloud and rainbows scattered
across the face of the hill.
New wheat and barley shake green
and silver ripples over the fields.
Bird, flower, insect, leaf, grass,
rise and fall and multiply, hatch
faster than beak or tooth can eat.

Summer is always hungry
moving out to catch the crop,
the mayfly hatch, the caterpillars
feasting on the new leaves,
unguarded nests, still ponds,
the nectar trail from orchard to lime walk,
from clover to heathery slopes,
cream, honey, berries, new eggs, love.

Occluded Front

The air is damp
as a wrung-out dishcloth.
Strawberries are swelling
squat under their pleated leaves.
Under a still and heavy sky
I pick the first gooseberries and hear
somewhere a skylark, pouring
her song into the barley field
under the gathering rain.

Pot Pourri

a rose alphabet
from alba semi plena
via gallica
to the thornless zephirine
writes my garden poem in
scent and scimitars

Bramble Barrens

The hedgerows are quieter now, the glitter
and flash of spring all gone to seed and only
the flossy gleam of meadowsweet to brighten
the clouds of buff and putty, drab and string shades
of flowers with mildly sinister names—
fools' parsley, hogweed, water dropwort.
It's a wallowing sea of moth and hoverfly
and this year's fledglings stripping the first berries,
squabbling and blundering through the grass.
The air is drowsy with heat and pollen,
thistledown and moulted feathers,
the bite of nettle sting and harvest mite.
A blackbird shakes a long rag of something
like a tablecloth, lays it straight and flat,
pecks and pecks, opening the brown flesh
of a yearling frog, while overhead drifts
the buzzard's wide lazy wing. Here there's just
one law. Remember your ass is lunch.

Sirius

The roses are done, the petal-tide
has ebbed, scented drifts browning
on the baked soil where harvestmen
stilt-walk after bug and aphid.

Chervil fades, and the spilled bloom
of meadowsweet dusts the pond.
Borage flaunts its black pincers
and pulsing traffic of bees.

The small apples show like beads
among stiff tarnished leaves.
We harvest tomatoes and berries
in the itch and sweat of summer.

Sunlight hits a blow to the head,
and the sky is molten, carved
by the screaming flight of swifts
round the steaming tenements.

This is August

The month of small green birds
blown like the turning leaves
between privet hedge and rowan,
weighting the slackwire stems
of meadowsweet over the pond.

The bat month, butterfly month,
month of hoverflies and junkie wasps
scoring a last sugar hit among the plums
and brambles. Month of scarlet rowans,
hips and haws, moths and spiderwebs.

Month of late orchids and heather,
of jags and prickles, drifting thistledown,
of dahlia flame, burning marigold flowers,
and tansy's brass-hard buttons,
all the hot metal flowers of the sun.

Month of wheat, heavy in the sullen fields,
aching for harvest like an unmilked breast,
a sudden wind, a thick dapple of cloud,
rain at the last in vindictive handfuls.

Revelry

Bees tumble, carousing to summer's end
in the flowers of borage and thyme
a frantic shimmer of brown and gold
over pink and purple cushions
and blue fallen stars in the grass.

Dawn

The pigeons swoop from the fire-warm
chimney to scavenge the early tarmac.
Sparrows have kept each other awake,
talking under the sycamore-leaf covers,
and a robin pulls an all-nighter
wired and singing in the lamplight.
On the mudbanks, sleeping mallards
are lifted by the slow swell of the tide,
bobbing like bath toys, heads still tucked
under the oblivion of their wings.

Dusk

Dusk comes softly over the stubble fields
and jackdaws leave river for cliff.
A fierce gold harvest moon
leaps and glowers over the hill
tangles itself in the long fading grass.

Wind Changing

A north-east wind rises, bringing with it
the rattle like promised rain of dry
birch leaves along the dusty pavement.

At night, ripe rain breaks like a wave
on the weathered shore of our slates.
Roof-beams creak and settle in their berths.

The crowded leaves of ash and beech disperse.
Light pours through rents in the orchard.
The world outside opens, comes closer.

Migrants

Sea-ducks are following the tide
up from Skinflats to Batterflats,
rolling and diving against the current
becoming acquainted with cold.
Abbot's Causeway to the Auld Brig,
and a kingfisher on the sallow
watches the meeting of burn and river
the place where salt meets fresh.
Gulls are gathering at the stones
dipping white wings. Sometimes
people wash up here, left at low tide
on the shallow bank, glazed with mud.

Lighting the Fire

Still winter evening.
The cloud on the hill drifts down
to meet the damp green on the grass,
the wet tarmac, disintegrating leaves,
despondent gardens.
Seeds and gardeners pause, withdraw,
frost outside, fire within.

Roof-Rider

The north wind batters into the house
and sucks the panes out of the greenhouse.
The slates above us clatter. The geese
are coming in long squadrons from the north
and leaves pile up against the door.
On the hearth the fire is quick to catch
but sullen walls clutch the hoarded cold
in dull corners whipped by draughts.
The imagined troll slick-sliding
from the wet and shuddering roof
takes, with the disintegrating slates,
all quiet, all safety, all hope of better.

Winter Webs

A spider spins diamonds
over the pile of leaves
blown into the porch.

She spins fractured glass
over the dark pool,
like bone, like crystal.
It grows like moss
over fallen branches
like lichen cascading
over the rock.

It softens, falls,
hardens and shatters,
breathes in, breathes out.
A web is spun
of melt and freeze
of inner glow,
of outer glitter,
stark nights, raw days.

Winter Settles In

Nine swans in a line
fly from orchard to causeway
in a fanfare of white wings

Fifteen long-tailed tits
trapezing on the birch stems
catching December sun.

A sky net unfurls
over the Forth's grey ripples—
starlings at sunset.

Dark wings against the snow—
two buzzards circle, harvesting
the dead of winter.

Mist on the river
heron stalks the reed beds
light grows, winter bites.

II

COVERED BY THE FOREST

I descend where all things
wild, the barking fox,
the wolf by grave, the ghosts
of dead, descend...

—Michael Hartnett from 'Secular Prayers'

Covered by the Forest

Morning light is softened beneath the trees
and the wind in the sycamore's high branches
moves the leaves like rain. I stop,
and the whole wood flickers around me,
precipitates the dawn chorus to flowers
of song, of dunnock, chaffinch, wren and thrush.
Cold and damp are nothing now, and I hear
the stealth of feeding and finding prey, the romp
of squirrel, weasel-screech, the scream of hawk.
Moss grows over my knees. Wings make passage
between the tangles of my spreading hair.
Beneath my buried feet, the push and flow
of water draws me inward. I grasp and shatter
rocks between my toes. The filaments of my roots
touch bluebell corm, cached acorns, badger's sett.
I do not flinch now from the small blows
of squirrel and treecreeper on my hardened skin;
ant and caterpillar are welcomed to my bark.
I sway with tides of moon and weather.
Sun and wind and rain speak world to me—
I hold it all in my wide-spread boughs.

Daphne

Her brother will inherit the land.
Her wealth is all in jewels, portable—
she won't be staying. Even her name
is temporary. His family will make her theirs.
Her mother tries not to get attached;
it isn't kind to let her put down roots.

She likes to be outside, escapes
from sewing, gossip, the family hearth.
Her friends are small birds on the reed-beds,
her love is pledged to field and tree.
When he comes, he'll have to snatch her,
she won't go with him, not if he was God.

She chooses well. She takes her stand
knee-deep in wet grass, her feet planted,
arms outspread like branches. She laughs
as bark encircles her, as flowers sprout
from finger-tips. She tastes her victory,
cries out as the green and stable earth
closes over her ecstatic head.

Land Speaks

Land speaks to the seed
of rock and sand and water
in the language of rush and heather,
taproots of trees and scavenging gorse.

Land speaks to the builders of nests
of wind and rain in the scour of river banks,
the burn's swift rush of water in the creeks,
the deep moss-cushions, the sway
of tall firs and the lie of wind blows.

Land speaks to the crawlers
of frost and sun, soft going and dry
in the bleached grass, and cracked seed-case,
the rise of small flies to the swallow's beak.

Land speaks to the trees
of growth and blossom and set seed
in the depth of pine needles on the forest floor,
decay of last year's leaves, and the green dust
of new seedlings on the wet mulch.

Land speaks to the buzzard
of running voles, and rabbits nibbling
the soft stems of clover and primrose flowers.

Land speaks to the bat
in lengthening days, warm nights,
of insects swarming, circling over the grass.

Land speaks of summer and winter
in the language of warbler and waxwing,
in rose and ivy flower, mist and lightning,
tree-rings, lichens and weathering stone.

Her Territory Marks

The river is full.
The cormorant
is up to his neck in it.

Cold broken heaps
of thin reed-flags
are retting in the mud.

Weep-holes in garden walls
let fall a thin slick
of hoarded rain.

The taint of fox breaks
into the chill and empty dawn
like a flung stone.

She Watches

In still October, the birch is spinning
gold from frost and sunlight.
Patio slabs are slicked and slippy.
The bird feeder gently swings in blue
and empty air. The grass is drenched.
A hanging spray of leaves has moved
without a wind, its jerks and twists
too far, too sudden, then stopped.
The hedge is still, taut as a held breath.
The sparrowhawk has landed.
Soundless, on the fence it's there—
a cream-and-cookies coloured scud.
It preens its ruffled feathers, scans
the ground. All quiet. Move on.

She Sleeps

This view is all of grooves. Raked clouds,
runrigs, sheep walks, and contour lines
like braided hair stretch to the horizon.

Hills slump, a rubble of broken teeth,
weathered wrinkles, nubs of rock, the fields
a lumpy pelt over discarded bones.

Plough-lines in the barley field
like fingerprints persist in the mould.
A wink of snow glints in the hedges.

Swellings, dimples, the sheen of new grass,
are long gone. She sleeps in a memory
of hefted sheep, spring squill, brown trout.

Huldra-Folk

Eve's unwashed children are hidden from God,
their less than pristine unruliness a blot
on her housewife's conscience. God knows.
He says, 'Let what is hidden, stay hidden.'
And so they are still, and we are enthralled to them,
to all that is elusive, estranged, entangled
in the structures where we think we live,
behind the skirting boards, under fingernails,
in the gullies and rhones and waste-pipes.
We strain for messages left in snail tracks,
deer scat, smudged footprints in the melting snow,
the ring of feathers at a kill-post, the rank
tarry, blood-and-wormwood scent of fox.
We think that we design the streets, the borders,
the kitchen gardens of our lives, clean
fertile places, productive, peaceful, known.
Yet all the while we know there lurks
a secret subversion, a lust for dark, a joy,
an outburst of untamed, unlicensed passion,
a living which goes on in spite of thought,
to which we are an interruption.

Nettle Shirt

In her mute pain, almost wilful, she sits
weaving shirts from nettles, sorting
peas from barley, beast-patiently
waiting to carry the strangers
over the mud at his door, walking
over knives, washing bloody shirts,
watching while he sleeps.

She remembers the brother
left with one swan-wing,
the blisters from the candlewax,
the careless word she spoke,
the butterfly wing broken
for haste, for fear, for greed.

Love, she might say, afterwards,
is content to wait the time,
to work through the slow laborious
process of restoration.

Love sees, but learns to sift
the loved from the loving,
the lie from the promise,
the wish from the walking.

Muse

Once they dreamed this,
the quiet domestic room
the lamp on the table where he will work,
the soft scrape of his pen
as it bleeds black ink
over the flat cream page,
the fireside chair where she will sew
and read, and check his proofs.
He will write her, she will read him.
They will be complete.

Now he to her is stone,
a tall rock, and she in its shadow,
she to him a thin high voice
constant, on the edge of hearing.
He to her is burden, she to him
is web. They no longer talk.
He has written her. She has read him.
They have eaten each other.

Marrying a Selkie

He knew she had this other life,
one he doesn't get, and never sees,
but he finds the traces sometimes—
a strand of seaweed in the shower,
the smell of salt, a silver scatter
of scales like sequins on the floor.
Women need a break sometimes
from all that domesticity.
He does not wonder where they go,
imagining their hair let down, their sleeves
bunched loosely up above their elbows,
bare feet dabbling in some rock pool.
No harm ever comes of it, his meal
will be on the stove to greet him
with the smell of herring, and the warm
fog of drying shirts and sheets.
He does not think he disapproves,
but all the same, on moonless nights
he thinks of women knitting, trays
of tea and scones, with rhubarb jam
blood red on flowered saucers,
and the sound of heads, soft-thumping
into baskets, while the needles click.

Away With the Fairies

For my mother

I wasn't away long, it couldn't
have been more than a week–
some nights, some days–I spent there.
And what I did there, it was too rich,
too many people, such scenes,
so much experience, so much going on,
the whole concern too much to tell you.
I was upset to see that grey-haired
old woman in the mirror, her sagging
cheeks and the old bat's glasses
and that wrinkled crook-toothed grin.

To me that summer is still today.
Leaving school rebellious, and laughing
and getting our jobs–June typing and filing
in the builder's office, Mary a nurse,
and Pat, who wants to travel, falling
for a baby, and marrying Stan,
and everyone scattered like chaff.
I'm the smart one, going to college,
there's books in my head, and music,
the smell of grass and pasta and candles.

That girl keeps telling me it was long ago.
She says I have grandchildren, and live here,
in some poky little house behind the park.
They've knocked Mam's house down now,
and built some shops, and the telly's rubbish.
She tells me John is dead.

At Skara Brae

I am at home here. The low roofs
are my height. I love the narrow streets
the dips in oil-filled oyster-shells, for light,
the water-stoops, the stone-built hearths,
the little sleeping-alcoves.

I built this house—or one the same—
in a wedge of post-war garden
between board fence and hedge of goldenrod
and crimson rambling rose,
with pillaged scaffold-planks, half-bricks,
old blackout curtains, orange boxes,
sheets of corrugated iron.

I built that stove, that kitchen dresser,
that counter like a saloon bar,
where cowboy brothers parked their guns
and caught imaginary liquor-glasses
I whizzed along the bar to waiting hands.

Now, in brick and concrete suburbs,
all buildings feel like play-houses,
and all machines are toys. And nothing
seems quite real but unforgiving wind,
red sun, hard rain, bare earth.

Christopher

The height of spring tide has left trash-lines
of winter-killed reeds and broken plastic.
In the drear of the morning, men in black
have come to drag the cold river,
raking the willow stems and fallen branches,
upending into the silty flow to grope
the lost bins and supermarket trolleys.
A horrible job, but worse to lift
the slack sodden weight of the boy.

And Christopher, a wink of cheap gold paint,
a dashboard puppet, swung key-fob, leans
wearily on his staff, the shouldered child
a weight too heavy in that storm,
the weight of the world's grief.

Runes for a New Millennium

After Havamal, from the Poetic Edda

I pulled all-nighters
to get the job done.
Between the Java and the Red Bull
I learned the fail-safe runes.

Know how to google them,
know how to download them,
know how to code them,
know how to encrypt them.

The first rune I know
is unknown to agony aunts,
therapists, life-coaches, counsellors.
Quick-fix it is called.

I know a second, that street-wise dudes
must learn if they want to be cool.

I know a third; when the going gets tough,
this will give me the edge.
This will see off the competition.

I know a fourth: when the shit hits the fan,
this rune will make sure
that nothing sticks to me.

I know a fifth; when I go into the meeting
no matter who is on the board,
I always close the deal.

I know a sixth; if I choose to use it,
when the merger happens, I will keep my job;
my rivals will all lose theirs.

I know a seventh, more powerful than any.
With this I will keep my figure
as strong and slim at sixty
as I was at sixteen.

I know an eighth, a gift for drivers.
With this I can always find parking space.
I have no fear of tickets.

I know a ninth; I can charm
the young and talented and beautiful
to find me irresistible.
My lovers will never leave me.

I know a tenth; when conscience racks me,
I can send guilt and remorse packing.
There are no skeletons in my cupboards.

I know an eleventh; the paparazzi
can get nothing on me.
No-one knows where my bodies are buried.

I know a twelfth, which I tell to no-one.
Age will make me good-looking.
Illness will be afraid to mess with me,
And death—what's that all about?

Wherever We May Find Her

For my father

I have seen her in old places in the countryside,
her statues in niches on French house walls,
under pointed wooden roofs at Irish crossroads,
and peering out of windows in the villages,
guarding the doorways of homes in Spain.

She watches my desk, looks out to sea
from the highest point at Ruabhal.
She is Our Lady of the Dew, Our Lady
of the Word, Our Lady of Long Fields,
the Good Mother of Marseilles,
who sails into port in her mantle of green,
Our Lady of the New Fire.

She is queen at Montserrat,
but also mountain, where women
call to neighbours in the mist, and young men
bring their brides to seal their marriages.
The Black Madonna, stiff and square,
sits in her carved brocade and lace,
the Christ-child seated on her knee,
the earth an orb in her cupped hand.
She is grimed with soot and candlesmoke
her toy world rubbed to the bare wood,
glossy with the touch of pilgrim hands.
The endless tourist shove and chatter
is halted when they reach her throne.
They pray, or maybe make a wish,
Stilled, for that short time, to peace.

She is remembered at nightfall,
and at the hour of death. At Rievaulx's
grass green ruins one sunlit afternoon
I heard her monks between the stones
sing *Salve Regina,* last hymn of the day.
We sang it too, the year before I married,
at summer school, and that is why,
that last hot August night, I sang again,
at your bed-side, to close your eyes:
O clemens, O pia, O dulcis virgo Maria.

Rewilding

This may be death, a gravelled grave-plot,
mown paths, and polished nameplates,
pristine, like the conifer's dry shade,
the parched soil, and the litter of acid
needles which never rot, but leave behind
a barren heap of nothing.

But in the house, moss grows soft
on the weathered slates, and at night,
the snail drags itself across the cool
of the stilled washing machine.
Slaters colonise the dusty space
behind the skirting boards, and mice
sharpen their teeth on the frayed pulp
of a doorframe on which three layers
of paint have chipped and peeled.

In the garden the sparrows establish
highways and tenements in the privet.
A hedgehog moves from pond to pond
through ruined larch lap fencing.
Swallows make their summer home
in shade where boards have fallen in.

This is not death, this timely passing away,
the long slow compost enriching the soil,
the quiet dismemberment of bones
leaching potash, the hair thatching nests.
This is the quiet repayment of debt—
dust to dust, ash returned to ashes,
life to the living.

Chant for the New Spring

Open the windows. Let sunlight
and laundered air breathe
through the dusty house.
Draw down water to thirsty roots.
Break the thin parchment
shrouding the dropped seed,
send new sprouts to drill,
and cling to the swaddling earth.
Tap on the shell till it cracks
and fill the nest with cheeps
and downy gaping beaks.
Let the small heart pump
colour into broad new wings
spread out to dry in the sun.
Let it grow, flower, sing, fly.

III

WALKING TO JERUSALEM

In order to arrive at that which thou knowest not
thou must go by a way that thou knowest not.

—St John of the Cross from *The Ascent of Mount Carmel*

Arriving in Glasgow

The drunk man rails at the statue.
Waste of space. Tosser. Fanny merchant.
Fanny merchant. Fanny merchant.
Dewar stares doggedly down the street.

Three boys film the skater who jumps
the railings on the ramp, meets the board,
crashes at the bottom of the steps.
He shakes his wrist. His knees are covered
with blood and bruises. He jumps again.

A Roma in a doorway plays
a Viennese waltz between the sounds
of blues guitar, and pipers down the street
riffing to cool Ghanaian drums.

Ten minutes later, the train departs.
Two phones deliver, 'I'm on the train.'
A blonde is marking up a text
on designing turbines. Across from me
the heavy metal dude takes out
his Fender, fills the air with sound.
Smoke on the Water. I'm almost home.

Habitation

This is a longhouse, a hut
knee-deep in damp, a runnel
separating bairns from cows.
It is made of found stones,
the first turf roof replaced
by red-painted corrugated iron.

There is not much inside.
The cluttered mantel holds the clock
and three prized flowery plates.
The cooking happens on the fire,
the bed in the recess sleeps three,
but there's a parlour kept decent
for the minister, the laird, a coffin.

But this is home, because
the flecked and rippled chestnut spars
that roof the byre shine red like light
filtered through closed eyelids,
because the blackened pot
always steaming on the hob
simmers to the stirrer's pulse.

The Place of the Fire

The right place for a fire
is a good place for a human—
dry and level beneath, air,
but not too much, and shelter
from wind and wet above.
It is safe where the fire is.

Glittering puffs of ignited smoke
drive ghost-pegs into the coal,
let out the prisoned light.
Soot-flags on the hearth-wall
welcome the stranger.
Later, the house walls sing with heat.

This brooding bird of a house,
its lintel a mossy breast-bone
we creep beneath, its walls stone wings
mantling our hearth-space where the fire's
warm quiver feeds us, guards us,
quickens what grows within.

Under parched and wasted coals,
the red glow dulls to night. The ash
settles softly, a quiet inward collapse
like the gentling of your face
on the pillow, as you fall
deeper into sleep.

Lost Village, Helmsdale

Here are come live with me hollows,
like the young seductive hills of Iceland,
their inclines catching the sun.
They are winter-burned, heather-bleached
to tephra-grey billows, an inland ocean.

No natural disaster ever came here,
No ash-cloud, fever, lava flow, but only
the suffocating tide of time,
of landlord's greed, want, hardship, cold.

Croft-house gable ends rise from the grass.
The hearths are cold and deep in moss,
sheep-walks and neighbour paths
ephemeral as breadcrumb trails.

The fields are gone to bracken,
wood sorrel, hidden primrose-banks.
The nettles still remember them,
in patches where the soil is deep and rich,
and skylarks, singing out their claim of right.

Lumb Bank

The bank is chisel cut between
stony sunlit plateaus. It's full of unlight,
unhope, neglect. They've all gone now
to quaint stone houses on the tops,
short on parking, but handy for the train.
Once fourteen sandstone mills
worked on the whorled grooves
of Colden Water's valley floor.
Between the ruins the quiet river idles.
The earth throws up a stand of sycamores
and clouds of himalayan balsam
pink between broken loom-shed walls.

Overlooking the Lake

The roads mirror hill contours. A slow-worm
stretches its bronze satin length
into the cool under the rock steps.
A bikers' conversation slides past
            —'which I felt quite sad about really,
but I knew not to mention it,
because I know how Hilary feels about it.'

Out on the lake, a cruiser makes way,
a steady lump of white amongst
the vertical lightness of dinghies,
slack-sailed, leaning into the cold slow drift
of an almost wind. Tree-tops beyond,
a spindrift of crimson bud-tips, a green sea
of new leaves, willow, hazel, thorn.

Grey Mug

I hold in my hands a grey mug,
one I never liked much, with its
blobby tube-lined bunch of grapes.
It was part of that time then, in Edinburgh,
when I was young and scared and hopeful
and ran about like a lapwing chick,
the shell still stuck on its silly head.
Everything was still to happen,
all my future was in my hands at last.
It is still here after thirty years.
I hold in my hands a grey mug
full of my unregarded past.

Steam and Hot Metal

The Waterford-Kilkenny railroad
brought them together. The peasants' fears
and prophet's warning of strange 'iron
carts that moved without horses'
whose 'first and last journeys would be
carrying corpses' didn't stop their marriage,
though they would lose five sons
in the smoke of Scotland Road.

Then he stoked boilers on the ships,
Dublin to Liverpool, and she came too,
left townlands for city, followed the steam
to Liverpool's back courts and dirt,
took in the Irish boys who came for work.
She washed their sheets, sent them to Mass
kept them and her four daughters
from drink, and (mostly) out of trouble.

Great-aunts would say I had the look of her,
and the way I'd twist my hair
reminded them of her. They winced.
In Grandma's house the kettle steamed
on the iron apron at the fire, and tea
was smoky, slacked and sweetened
with conny-onny from a tin, not milk.

She never talked of Ireland, of her time
in exile at the farm to cure TB.
For fifty years, she washed her coins
the way they taught her, to prevent the spread
of white plague, with its taint of filth.

Her hands were soft, and slippery as silk,
hot-water worn—as mine are now,
so my own grand-daughter says.

In the Church

Descendant, he once told me, from Grace O'Malley,
the Irish pirate queen, the little Irishman
bustles the laggards in to church. Now he dusts,
with a handkerchief from his pocket,
the statues of St Joseph, the Little Flower,
St Anthony who cuddles Baby Jesus,
and, standing on the spilled intention cards,
the one he needs most of all, St Jude.

In the quiet after Mass, the heavy scent
of someone's wedding lilies blends
with paraffin from night-lights on the stand
winking red and blue. Twin grooves
score the treacly varnish of the pews,
where children, unobserved, cut second teeth,
and pick the blebs of candle wax from Easter.

In the sanctuary, a constant flame
flickers and remains, like who he is,
when conversation fails, and memory,
and all he knows, dusting familiar statues,
is here, the last place where he is known.

After Visiting Time

Through the double doors
that lead to the locked ward
the old man walks whistling,
a blackbird lilt, sweet and tuneful.
His pale wife leans on his arm,
trusting him to keep her steady.
No need to talk; they take
an easy pace. The door shuts,
swinging behind them like a scythe.
He comes back solo, whistling still.
He needs the comfort now.

Hugh's Farewell to Arms

The end came in the Japanese camps.
We thought it was all over, and we'd won.
And then they sent us to Korea
to bring the prisoners home. I held him,
a man of six feet, dying in my arms
lighter than a ten year old boy.

That was enough for me. They sent
a letter with some forms to apply
for all the medals we had earned—
Dunkirk, the Shetland Bus, the work with
Lovat Scouts, the D-Day landings—I thought
of all those silly Canadian boys,
dead before they'd got their boots wet,
too young, too curious, too ill-trained
to keep their heads down as we came in.

I put the letter on the back of the fire.
I said 'We've achieved nothing. I've got
five sons of my own at home,
and I'm coming back to make pacifists
out of the lot of them!' I'm glad to hear
your daughter's joined the CND. Tell her
from me—keep up the fight!

War Hero to Me

He was no child's idea of a war hero,
quiet and polite, inclined to be grumpy,
stumping along with his stick
and his thick old man's glasses.

He shared a house with a pal,
in a relationship no-one would mention
until it was legal. They kept themselves
to their quiet selves until he fell ill.

He told visitors then of the Great War
his time in the Royal Flying Corps,
when he'd been magnificent, a flighty
young experimenter in the new planes.

He'd dodged the anti-aircraft guns,
flew blind in bad weather, carried
untested weapons, learned to fight
a whole new way of making war.

'They'd load us up with bombs', he said.
'and send us over the Channel to bomb
strategic targets, and anything else below.
No such thing as non-combatant then.

We'd find a quiet field with no houses,
and let them all go, fly home and say
nothing to anyone. You couldn't go round
dropping things like that on people!'

Sea-Henge

On that far wall
four blank slabs of light.
On this, the window shows
a sapling ash, bare-limbed,
black buds not yet breaking,
clutched tight against the blue
stealth of a sullen spring.

The years have flowed like the sea
over these withered bones,
uprooted and laid out
between sheets of cold linen.
They bear the weight of memory,
the lovers, the children,
grassy play-times, ink-stained desks,
the fall of governments, music,
the planting of gardens.

The years have flowed like the sea
over the henge in the saltmarsh,
the alder carr over the bog,
peat building over the alders,
the sand over the peat,
and, over the sand, the sea.

I wait for the tide and a wind
screaming with gull-cries
to take me out between the layers
between memory and reflection,
between the glass and the light.

Burial Rites

Grave Kist

Sand and storm protected, then revealed
this clutch of homes, so distant from us,
a settlement where tern and bonxie
are more at home than hens and sheep,
where seal and limpet matter more than kye.
Once their dead were among them, in safe places.
Owl and otter lived in the kists after,
and now strangers walk over the dunes,
to peer at cold stones through glass.

Grave Goods

After the funeral they come to the green,
four young men and the widow. They stand
a while, talking softly, then go, leaving
the wreaths and the photos, and the things
he'll need, or he'll miss where he's gone—
a Guinness candle, a long bright can of beer,
a plastic-covered Tesco's apple pie.

Walking to Jerusalem

Footsore and hungry, our hands full
of cockleshells, crucifixes, wayleaves,
distracted by forest hermitages,
by abbeys and basilicas, and archetypal
marshes and wilderness.

Next year, next year, and the wine in the glass cups
thin and sour, and no honey left.
The dogged one foot after another,
driven or drawn. We lost sight
of need behind us, desire ahead.

The road, the dust, the cold at night, the shade of olives.
Scents of resin, of hyssop and sage,
holm-oaks in the courtyards and the sound
of fountains behind white walls.
The dogs at the road ends.

Dreaming of water in the green grass,
mud and sap and leaf back there, the white
and yellow honey scent of meadows,
cress and the flicker of willow leaves.

City of light, city of slaughter.
Not one stone standing on another.
Not this, not that; neither here nor yonder.
The place where God lives. Shalom.
Salaam. The place that breaks your heart.

Acknowledgements

Thanks are due to the editors of the following publications where many of these poems first appeared: *Drey, Eildon Tree, Northwords Now, Poetry Scotland,* and *Southlight,* in the online publications *Catapult to Mars, New Linear Perspectives, The Stare's Nest, Stravaig, YorkMix* and *Zoomorphic,* and in the anthology *Dark Mountain* Volume 3. The poem *Sea-Henge* was part of the StAnza exhibition in the Byre in 2012. 'Christopher' was commended in the William Soutar Competition in 2013. 'Northern Stones' won the Poetry Scotland Haibun Competition in 2015.

Thanks are due to The Gallery Press for permission to reprint the following: lines from 'Helplessness' by Kerry Hardie first appeared in *Only This Room* (2009) and are included in *Selected Poems* (2011). Lines from 'Secular Prayers' by Michael Hartnett appear in *Collected Poems* (2001).

Lines from *The Ascent of Mount Carmel* have been taken from the translation of E. Allison Peers published by Burns & Oates (1935).